BROOKLYN
REVOLT
and other narrative poems

NUBIA

This is a work of creative nonfiction. The events and conversations in this book have been set down to the best of the author's ability, although some names and details have been changed to protect the privacy of individuals.

Copyright © 2021 by Nubia

All rights reserved. No part of this book may be reproduced or used in any manner without written permission of the copyright owner.

First edition

Book Design and Graphics by Jordan Hughes

ISBN: 9798595764704

Imprint: Independently Published

Dedication

To my parents:
Thank you for your unconditional love;
without you there would be no me.

To my husband and son:
Thank you for loving me for me.

To my family:
Thank you for investing and believing in me.

Author's Note

We all experience challenges in life, we are silenced by some, others we revolt and rise against. Brooklyn Revolt is a collection of narrative poems written over three decades, that records my life in Brooklyn, New York. Thank you for joining me on this poetry journey. Thank you for rising with me. I hope you experience some laughter and tears in the verses of the narrative poems that follow. I hope you are also inspired to rise against and overcome your own challenges in life. We are all rising in our own way. We are all a revolt.

Table of Contents

Part Four

Young Heartbreak

Part 5

Peddy

Brooklyn Revolt

Part Six
Brooklyn Revolt

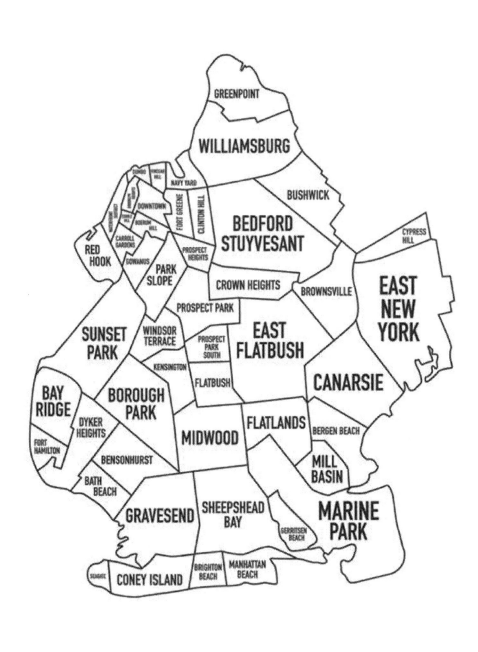

Part One

Home

Brooklyn, New York, has been my home for most of my life. My earliest memories of home include morning rides with my mother on the train to my elementary school. My mother is in her late 20s, and she sits close to me while we commute on the "A" train from Far Rockaway, Queens, to Bedford Stuyvesant, Brooklyn. Far Rockaway was one of my brief homes, but it was no Brooklyn. It's the late 90's and there are no cell phones or tablets, so we are actually talking, and she is sharing stories about her childhood with me. I love hearing these stories. My mother's family lives in Bedford Stuyvesant or "Bed Stuy" as we call it. During my childhood, it is a community filled with families of color who live in gorgeous brownstone homes, corner stores where you can purchase a quick snack of chips and a juice for 50 cents, and grandmothers sitting outside on the stoops watching their grandchildren jump Double Dutch and play tag. Gentrification has resulted in the neighborhood being called Stuyvesant Heights, as Caucasian people started to dominate the community, leading to increased rents and the displacement of minority homeowners. Coffee shops quickly replaced corner stores. It's always going to be Bed Stuy to us. My mother's family lives on Halsey Street, which is about four blocks away from my elementary school. We get off at Utica Avenue train station and walk together through Fulton Park. I notice the different colored leaves of fall on the trees in the park. I look up at my mother. She has dark skin and her hair is always in long braids. She is petite with beautiful bright eyes and a loving smile. To me she is the most beautiful woman in the world and just walking next to her feels like home.

My parents met as teenagers before ending their relationship when I was a child. At my birth she was 16 and he was 19. She is from a family from Alabama who immigrated to New York. He is an immigrant from Grenada, the Caribbean Isle of Spice, whose mother died of cancer when he was only 6. I was the result of their young love- an Afro Caribbean girl who would be immersed in both the African American and Caribbean cultures. As my parents attended college I would be looked after by various uncles and aunts. My dad's youngest sister played a large part in raising me. I was always welcomed into her home until she gave birth to her own son and out of some jealousy, I imagine, I attempted to strangle him with the telephone cord of his toy phone. I eventually adjusted to sharing my aunt so it became easy for me share my parents. I was an only child for six years before both my parents settled down, married, and had additional children. Suddenly I had a set of stepparents and became the oldest of my seven siblings combined between my mother and father. Spending time with each of my siblings felt like home.

My earliest memories of my dad include rides in his '88 Toyota Cressida with its gray cloth seats. "Dangerously" by Barrington Levy is playing from his car CD player. He is tall with small dreads in his head and a loud laugh. There is no air conditioner in his car. It is summer in Brooklyn, and I am hot. We're driving to visit relatives in Brownsville, Brooklyn. Brownsville is a community comprised of families of color. My relatives own large multi-family homes with space for me to run in the backyard and play with my cousins to the music of Beres Hammond, Sanchez, and Beenie Man. Brownsville is about a 20-minute drive from Bed Stuy. We always grab McDonalds. I am enjoying the drive and the breeze from the open car window is providing some relief from the heat. Just being in my dad's presence, feels like home. The poetry that follows depicts this young Afro- Caribbean girl's diverse experience with her parents, her family, and her home, written from the eyes of a young child.

My Mother

Put my Mother on the $100 bill.

Let everybody see her smile.

Let her know she's loved and good at everything she does.

Put my Mother on a coin,

Not a dime or a penny,

She's worth more,

Actually,

She's worth plenty.

Why?

You ask, should all this be done?

She's just a Mother and everyone has one.

Actually,

My Mother is more than a mom,

She's a sister,

She's a cousin, daughter, and someone's true love.

She can be a dad,

She can be mean. At times, she can be sweet and very nice.

My Mother,

Has been through much but still exceeded in life.

She should be a monument,

For all that she's been through,

This is what I dream should happen,

I wonder if it will come true…

My Mother should have a flower named after her called "Hope"

With this flower called "Hope", the world would cope.

It would have colors like purple,

orange and green, blue, brown, violet and red too.

My Mother,

A statue standing,

She'd be very tall in Washington, DC.

A big smile and pretty eyes,

Everyone passing by would see.

Make her birthday a holiday,

Celebrate at least,

Everyone should have a very big feast.

See…

My Mother is one in a million!

Actually, she's one in a billion!

She should be remembered for all that she has been through,

And all that she continues to be…

My Mother,

My Queen,

I pray her future is stress-free.

My Daddy

My Daddy…
Is a man of few words,
He is as cool,
As the fall breeze.

My Daddy…
Is admired by many,
He is loved by his family,
He is especially loved by me.

My Daddy…
Is a superhero.
Always rescuing me
From my fears and from my tears.

He is always protecting me,
He tells me, "Stop wearing your heart on your sleeve!"
And constantly reminds me that he loves me unconditionally.

My Daddy…
Is one of my best friends.
Always cracking jokes with me,
He asks me questions,

He gets honest answers,
There are no secrets kept.

Laughing together for best,
Crying together for worse,
My Daddy and I are very close.

Cigarettes

They make her breath smell badly.
They stop her from becoming mad.

She smokes them.
They help ease her stress.
She believes no one understands.

She walks into the kitchen.
Lights one using the stove.
Smokes it in the bathroom.

She doesn't want to be disturbed when she smokes,
She smokes because she's grown.
She's grown and can do whatever she pleases- is what she reminds me.
She smokes them to calm down.

She smokes them when she feels bad.
But what she doesn't know is that she's making me, her child, feel mad.

And won't she feel sad,
When she finds out that these things can make her sick?

She thought they were good in the moment,

But they're bad for her over time,

But...

She's addicted,

She can't stop,

She smokes a lot,

She's a victim to the cigarette,

It makes her feel free.

When she first started smoking as a teenager, she probably felt glee,

After the first time there was no rewind,

It seems like she's smoking forever,

I hope it doesn't end up this way,

I hope in the end that she is okay, and she throws her last cigarette away.

Legacy

8 children.

5 girls.

3 boys.

They grew up to be strong women and men.

To smile through challenging times.

They all have the same eyes,

But different complexions of skin.

They are different shades of black.

And growing up-they always had each other's back.

They were all born in the West Indies.

Grenada is where you gave them life.

Your youngest was 6 when you passed away of cancer

And made your transition to the afterlife.

And he immigrated to America so young,

With your daughter and sons, his siblings.

They took care of him like he was their own son.

Made sure he had clothing, food, shelter,

That he graduated from college and earned his degree in architecture.

He would join the army and later in life he would become a sergeant in the NYPD.

He had no memories of you-grandma- he became a father at 19.

His family soon become larger; he became a parent of 4 kids.

His first child was raised with the help of his sibling, your youngest daughter.

Why did she do it?

Love,

Grit and Persistence,

It's what you taught them,

It's what I now see.

It's the importance of sticking together,

The importance of family.

Your children and grandchildren will forever hold you in their memories and hearts.

To the grandmother I never met...

Thank you for you,

Thank you for my aunts,

Thank you for my uncles too.

Thank you for your youngest daughter and son-my daddy.

Marjorie, thank you for me.

Part of you is within me.

Nubia.

I am your legacy.

Grandma

A young girl born in Tuskegee.

With a heart of gold.

You worked hard as the granddaughter of a sharecropper.

You picked cotton as a child and did as you were told.

Your family didn't have much but they made do.

You followed your mother to New York City and then you graduated from high school.

Between a rock and a marriage, you gave birth to 6 kids.

3 girls.

3 boys.

They grew to be resilient women and men.

They experienced a lot in life but didn't let that defeat them.

They saw that you had challenges too but you didn't stop no matter the reason.

You pushed through your divorce,

As a single mom,

You went back to school and found a city job,

A way to support your family,

Purchased a home in Bed Stuy,

A place where everyone could stay,

You never turned family or friends away.

Lived in the city but still a Tuskegee, Alabama, country girl, at heart.

You're a survivor.

You experienced the loss of your father, the loss of your son, the loss of your brother and most recently the loss of your mother.

But you never stopped growing.

You published a book and started your own business in retirement.

Supported your late son's children.

You helped everyone when needed.

You are-you- no matter the season.

Against adversity you stay strong and are never defeated.

To the only grandma I've known...

You continue to show me how to be.

How to face challenges in life.

Thank you for my mom, my aunts, my uncles, and thank you for me.

Thank you for always supporting and loving our family.

Why?

Why didn't you take me?

Why couldn't I have went?

Why did I have to stay here?

Why did you leave me alone again?

Why Do I Cry?

Why do I cry?
Don't the tears ever get tired of running down my face?

Why do I cry?
Doesn't my heart ever get tired of feeling so much pain?

Why do I cry?
Why can't bad memories just go away?

Why do I cry?
Why can't I just think straight?

Why do I cry?
Why can't my Mother come visit me?
Why does my Dad have to be away in the Army?

Why do I cry?
Why do I feel like I don't have a home without my parents near?
Why do I feel like nobody cares?

Why do I cry?
Why can't I go to sleep?

Why do I cry?

Somebody please tell me why my soul can't have peace.

They Say

They say they see a future for me...

They say they see me arguing with authority.
They say they see me pregnant as a teen.
Is that what's in the future for me?

They say they see me so sad.
They say I'm not going to make it in life.
They say I talk too much.

What shouldn't I say?
What should I do?

They say I'm a bookworm but I have no sense.

They say I have problems.

They say they see me...

What family is this supposed to be?

They say I don't need a bath,
I bathe three times daily and they don't understand why.
Maybe I'm trying to clean my body real hard so I won't feel so dirty,

And invaded,

It may have been a year so far,

But it still feels like it was yesterday.

They say they are going to ban me from the bathroom.

They lock me out of my own home and sometimes they don't let me in.

I'm outside in the cold and I'm alone.

They say I don't have a true home.

They say many things about me.

Is this what you call my family?

Beauty

I am beautiful because my mother is beautiful,

Because my father is beautiful,

Because I am of my mother and father.

I am beautiful because my grandmother is beautiful,

Because I am of my grandmother.

I am beautiful because I am loving,

I am beautiful because I am caring,

I am beautiful because I am me.

I am beautiful because I am strong.

Because I am African American and Grenadian.

Because I am from a family of immigrants from the West Indies.

And a family that migrated from the South.

Because my family were sharecroppers in the south and they still made it out.

Because my ancestors were slaves who were strong and resilient.

Because despite experiencing challenges in life I remain persistent.

My beauty is defined by my mere existence.

Home

Home
Where it's comfortable.
You can easily fall asleep
On any bed.

Home
Where nothing's nicely said.

Home
No secrets are kept.

Home
A very warm environment.

Home
Peaceful and quiet and loud.

Home
No matter what block,
What house,
It is still my home.
Where I have my family.
A room I share with my siblings.

My bed.

A good place to rest my head.

I know no matter what happens or

How my day ends....

I will still be able to go home.

Part Two

Childhood Trauma

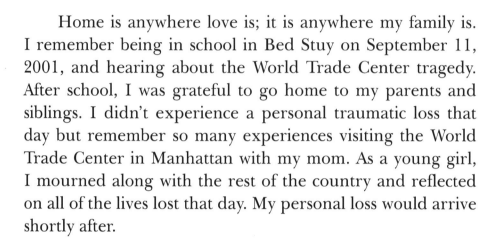

Home is anywhere love is; it is anywhere my family is. I remember being in school in Bed Stuy on September 11, 2001, and hearing about the World Trade Center tragedy. After school, I was grateful to go home to my parents and siblings. I didn't experience a personal traumatic loss that day but remember so many experiences visiting the World Trade Center in Manhattan with my mom. As a young girl, I mourned along with the rest of the country and reflected on all of the lives lost that day. My personal loss would arrive shortly after.

Surprisingly, it was a loss that I would experience at my new home in Flatbush, Brooklyn. We recently relocated to Flatbush after leaving Far Rockaway, Queens. At the time Flatbush was a community largely filled with families of color who lived in mixed apartment buildings and multi-family or single-family homes. We lived in a large affordable housing apartment complex across the street from my aunt. The complex was then called "Vanderveer Estates" and was once plagued by violence. Like Bed Stuy and so many other neighborhoods in Brooklyn, gentrification has also occurred in Flatbush and "Vanderveer" is now "Flatbush Gardens."

It was a hot summer day and the school year was almost over. I would be a 5th grader in September and was looking forward to my first prom and graduation.

My mom woke me up at 6am. She was on her way to work and today I was not going to school. My little sister was staying home with me. My stepfather walked into our home five minutes later. He had been out all night, and I was scared of staying home alone with him and my little sister. He struggled with substances, and after two years in rehab he still hadn't recovered from his addictions.

My mom was planning to leave him and I couldn't wait until she did. My mom must have sensed how I was feeling because she started calling my aunt and other relatives asking if we could stay with them for the day. They said "No," with excuses like "I'm busy." With no other options my mom was forced to leave me at home with stepfather. This was a decision she would later regret.

I fell asleep and when I woke up, he was in my face with a knife. All I remember thinking was 'What in the hell is he doing?'

I asked him, "What are you doing?"

"Don't scream," he said.

I started to cry because I knew something terrible was about to happen to me. I was so terrified. I was in danger. Flight, fight, or freeze? I'm a runner at heart. I ran to the door but he blocked my way.

"Don't try that again." he said.

Still holding the knife, he shoved me into the bedroom that he shared with my mother.

"Take off your clothes," he ordered once we were alone in the bedroom.

I did as I was told.

"You're just as beautiful as I imagined." he said.

I looked at him in disgust. I was so afraid. I didn't know if he would kill me. He told me to get on the bed and I did. Then he got on top of me. I felt instant pain between my legs. I felt tears running down my face.

"You know I've been waiting to do this for a long time," he said.

I tried to make conversation so he wouldn't kill me. It seemed like a good idea at the time.

"Why?" I asked.

He didn't respond. I started to panic. I couldn't talk anymore. I was relieved when he finally stopped but it wasn't over. He used me in other ways sexually. I felt disgusted. When he was satisfied, he got up and left the room. I wanted to run but I felt paralyzed and I couldn't move. I mustered the strength to get dressed.

"You cannot tell anyone what happened, if you tell anyone, I'll kill your mother and your brother and sisters," he said.

"I won't tell!!" I yelled while still crying.

I wanted to leave the apartment, but he wouldn't let me, so I told him I needed to get my radio from my aunt's house across the street. This was a time where radios were as important as a cell phone is today. He made me call her first on the landline while he watched in front of me. I dialed her number as fast as I could. She picked up after the second ring.

"Hello," she answered in a sleepy voice.

"Aunty, I'm coming to get my radio," I said.

"No, my house is dirty!" she yelled.

"Okay, I'm coming over, bye." I quickly hung up.

I turned to face him and said my aunt agreed that I could come over.

"Well don't tell her." he reminded me.

"Okay." I nodded with conviction and left the apartment.

I quickly ran across the street and knocked heavily on my aunt's door. When she opened the door, I just fell on the hardwood floor and broke down sobbing.

"Nubia, what happened?" she asked.

"He raped me!" I yelled.

"What?" I could see the tears in her eyes.

"He raped me!" I yelled again.

She called my mother and told her what had happened to me. She also called my great uncle, my late grandfather's brother, for support. He arrived shortly after and we all went back to my apartment together to pick up my little sister who was still sleeping in her bedroom. We acted normal. As we left the apartment with my sister, the cops walked in and arrested him. I couldn't look him in his face.

"Somebody should go in there and kick his ass!" my great uncle yelled.

The cops calmed him down. As we walked to the ambulance, I called my dad to tell him what happened and I started to cry. I was a daddy's girl that now felt violated. My dad and mom met me at Kings County Hospital where I was being examined. My mom held me and started crying.

"He's going to pay!" she said repeatedly.

I just cried and reflected on my early morning train rides with her from Far Rockaway to Brooklyn on the A train. One morning she shared her story of being sexually assaulted by her uncle when she a child. Later I discovered that it was my great uncle who said "somebody should get in there and kick his ass." He had sexually assaulted my mother when she was about my age. I thought to myself, 'I guess it's true what they say: like mother, like daughter.' Some mothers and daughters share birthday months or favorite colors. My mom and I were now both victims of childhood sexual assault. It's not the experience you'd want to have in common with your mother or anyone else for that matter. It's an experience I wouldn't wish on anyone. I looked at my mother and all that she had achieved in life despite her childhood trauma. I knew this experience would change my life, but like my mother, I would not be defeated by it. It would become a part of my being, a piece of me that would help shape me into the woman I was meant to be. The short poems that follow depict my experience, written as a child, with the community trauma of WTC and how I felt about my own personal trauma of sexual assault.

On That Very Awful Day

When I think of that awful day...

My whole perspective begins to change, because I thought it was just an ordinary day.

People went to work.

Kids went to day care.

Customers went to shop at the World Trade Center.

On that very awful day...

Terrorists hi-jacked a plane,

They crashed into the World Trade Center, and so many lives were changed.

On that very awful day...

Children lost their parents,

Parents lost their children,

Sisters lost their brothers,

Brothers lost their sisters.

On that very awful day...

Cousins lost their cousins,

And husbands lost their wives,

Wives lost their husbands, and many people lost their lives.

On that very awful day people's lives were not the same.

On that very awful day, the world cried and prayed,
For the innocent people that passed away,
On
That
Very
Awful
Day.

If I Could Change the Time

If I could change the time,
Happiness would be mine.

If I could change the time,
Everything would be fine.

If I could change the time,
Maybe I wouldn't have been assaulted.
Maybe my body could still feel like mine.

If I could change the time,
Maybe I wouldn't have had a door slammed in my face,
Maybe when people ask me how I am doing, I could honestly say, "I am feeling great!"

If I could change the time,
Maybe I would do better in school.
My teachers say I could do better if only I knew how to follow rules.

I wouldn't be crying all the time,
If I could change the time.

Part Three

Teenage Self-Reflection

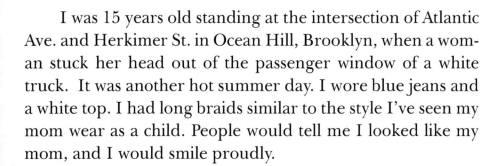

I was 15 years old standing at the intersection of Atlantic Ave. and Herkimer St. in Ocean Hill, Brooklyn, when a woman stuck her head out of the passenger window of a white truck. It was another hot summer day. I wore blue jeans and a white top. I had long braids similar to the style I've seen my mom wear as a child. People would tell me I looked like my mom, and I would smile proudly.

"You are so beautiful!" the woman yelled. She was African American with a friendly smile.

I was raised to be polite. "Thank you," I responded.

"With your beautiful body and face, I would be able to get you nice things, clothes, and a lot of money. Come in my truck, and we can talk about it some more."

Flight, fight, or freeze? The traffic signal changed at the intersection. I'm a runner at heart. I ran as quickly as I could so that I could get away from her. If somebody was going to attempt to kidnap me, they would have to catch me first. I only stopped running when I was safe at a friend's house. We talked about the incident. My mother, who briefly moved to Virginia with my siblings, had permanently returned to New York. My father was a solider in the Iraq war.

This incident could have been the perfect ingredients of a recipe for disaster, but I immediately thought about the last time I heard an adult comment on my young, developing body. I could see my stepfather holding me hostage in my mother's room with a knife, looking at me with lust in his eyes. This woman was attempting to sexually traffic me, and I am grateful that I was able to get away from her. I didn't realize it at the time but my body had responded to this dangerous situation without me even thinking about it.

My traumatic experience with childhood sexual assault changed the course of my life in so many ways. It helped me get away from this dangerous woman, because I was always on alert and looking for signs of danger. I was diagnosed with Post Traumatic Stress Disorder. I didn't talk to anyone about my feelings, but I wrote poetry often. The following poems depict a young teenage girl's effort at self-reflection.

I Say

I say it started when I got assaulted.
Afterwards my happiness just halted.

It stayed with me.

Haunting and taunting.

It's a nightmare that comes back and interrupts my dreams.

A nightmare that makes me scream
"Somebody, help me please!"

Nobody Knows

Nobody knows…
How I feel inside,
And all the feelings I hide.

Nobody knows…
That I cry at night.

Nobody even knows…

Why?

I don't know why I feel this way and why these feelings won't go away.
Sometimes I wonder, are these feelings here to stay?

Nobody knows…
How lonely I am,
I feel like I don't have any real friends.

Nobody knows all the pain I go through,
And all the pain that stays.

Nobody knows the real me,
I'm just a mirror image of everything I see.

Tears

I cry tears of pain.

Tears in vain.

I cry tears of joy.

I cry tears for you, tears for me.

Tears for my whole family.

I cry tears at night.

I cry tears, and I wonder why.

Why can't things be alright?

My tears come from within.

When I can't hold them in, they burst out and then
The tears slowly come down my eyes and…
I
Just
Can't
Stop
Crying.

She Is

She is 5'5".
Boys say she has a "fat ass,"
With skinny legs,
And thick thighs,
She's oh so fine!

Slim stomach,
Big breasts,
Beautiful eyes.
She's oh so fine!

With that brown weave,
Long and curly,
She knows she's worthy.
You don't have to tell her she's beautiful.
She doesn't need a boy to boost her ego.
Her skin is as dark as the women in Rio.
She's oh so fine!

She's smart and funny,
Does her best in school.
Her smile brightens up the room.
She's oh so cool.

Who is she?
A good person is who she is,
With a heart of gold,
The body of a goddess,
The face of a Nubian Princess.

Boys don't play with her mind,
Please don't waste her time,
Because she's oh so fine!

Nubia

When I think of Nubia...

I remember a whole lot of Nubias.

I remember the Nubia who loved her daddy to death,

Who always liked going to his house every weekend,

Who loved him picking her up from home and heading to Pizza Hut or IHOP.

The Nubia who loved her beautiful mother with the beautiful name.

The mother who she looked up to and wanted to be.

The mother who hustled to care of 5 children on her own.

The Nubia who wrote stories and poems and Dragon Ball Z fanfiction.

The Nubia who said she'd never like a boy.

The Nubia that always wore her afro in the summer and loved how it looked.

The Nubia who was a self-proclaimed tomboy.

The Nubia who liked drama and wanted to be an actress.

The Nubia who got sexually assaulted.

The Nubia with an attitude.

The Nubia who was very sensitive and cried for everything.

I remember the Nubia who said she'd never get her heart broken...

And I remember the Nubia who did.

Part Four

Young Heartbreak

My experiences with trauma left me alerted and aware of physical danger as a teen, but I was not alerted or aware of the importance of emotional danger, of protecting my teenage heart. My emotions were like a rollercoaster, and I could not get off the ride to protect my young heart from experiences with young heartbreak. It all started with my first kiss.

It was November 2003 and the weather outside in Crown Heights, Brooklyn, was chilly. The wind was heavily blowing, but my friends and I did not want the day to end. There was no Facebook, Twitter, or Instagram at this time. If we wanted to gossip, vent about our day and build our friendships, we had to spend time together outside, even if the weather was cold. We purchased snacks from the corner store—chips, juice, and shared packs of Winterfresh spearmint gum. We then went to Lincoln Terrace Park. I sat on a bench while my first boyfriend sat next to me. We were classmates in school, but after school we were just two teenage kids sitting on a bench.

He brought me Valentine's Day cards and little chocolate bars. We wrote each other "love letters" in class. He put his arm over my shoulders as we sat on the bench on that cold fall day. I cannot remember what we talked about. We stopped in the middle of the conversation and looked at each other. We moved a little closer together. My heart skipped a beat before our tongues entwined. There was a sour ending to that beginning, a sour ending—to that sweet first kiss. My first heartache would be born on this park bench, and a few short years later, my heart would break in pieces at Canarsie Pier. The following poems embrace a young teenage girl's experiences with young heartbreak and all she learned about young love, from the park benches and piers in Brooklyn.

Love

Love…

What is the meaning of this world you say?

I don't know…but would it brighten up my day?

Am I supposed to feel this way?

When love comes my way…

Will I be swept off my feet?

And too excited to sleep?

Would I want to stay up on the phone with him all night?

When he has to go, would I start to cry?

Would it be like what I see on TV and the things I read?

I'm looking for love,

Mind-bending,

Heart-thumping,

Soul-stirring,

Love.

Sometimes I get confused.

I hear this word often used.

People say it all of the time.

I don't understand it or what it means.

I think I fell in love, but I really don't know.

Is there a meaning?

Are there ways I can see...is he really the one for me?

I'm looking for love,
Mind-bending,
Heart-thumping,
Soul-stirring,
Love.

Is love that feeling you get in your stomach?

Is love like planting a seed?

Will it grow like a flower into something more?

Through sickness and health, till death do us part...

After saying these words, will you be together forever, or will your relationship just fall apart?

If I love someone and I'm not loved back...

Would it hurt inside?

Would it make me cry?

I'm looking for love,
Mind-bending,
Heart-thumping,
Soul-stirring,
Love.

I don't know what to think…
Suddenly I'm feeling weak.
Is this love?
I cannot see.
Let me talk to love,
Maybe love will understand me.

Love,
I want to know what you mean.
I'm starting to feel my heart beat.
There's a person who can make it beat fast and slow at the same time.
Is this even possible?
I have no idea.

I feel love coming
Feels like it's near…

L to the O almost to the V to the E.

Love, you're here.
Love, you're here.
Love, please don't hurt me.
Love, please don't hurt me.

I've found love,
Now my mind is bending,
My heart is thumping,
And my soul is stirring,
Because I am in love.

'

I Don't Know

I don't know much about me,
But I know with you is where I want to be.

I don't know much about art,
But I know you and I make a perfect picture.

I don't know much about astronomy,
But I know you are my shining star.

I don't know much about history,
But I know my future will include you and me.

I don't know much about math,
But I know you + I = perfection.

I don't know much about science,
But I know you make my heart swell.

I don't know much about health,
But I know when I'm sick and I call you, I feel well.

I don't know much about gym,
But my hands start to sweat around you.

I don't know much about me,

But I know with you is where I want to be.

All Because

Blood rushing through my veins.

Feeling so much pain.

Needing every white blood cell's protection.

Pointing out all of my imperfections.

Going through these up and downs.

Feeling sad when you're not around.

Crying late at night because you're not treating me right.

I *feel* like I am going crazy!

Naw, it's true;

I **am** going crazy,

And it's all because of you.

Difficult

It's so difficult to look at you and not cry.

It's so difficult to look in your eyes.

It's so difficult to see you with her.

It's so difficult to deny that our relationship is over and through..

It's so difficult to not be able to feel the touch of your hug,
And to not have you around,
And for you to ignore me as if I was a speck on the ground.

After all we've been through…
It's so difficult to not be with you.

Cup of Tea

You are my cup of tea.
Bitter, but sweet.
Hot, sometimes cold.

Black,
Southern,
Green,
Different varieties.
They're like different versions of you.

You are my cup of tea.
You warm my soul on cold days.
When I'm sick you help my flu go away.
You're soothing and help ease my sore throat.

I don't know what I would do without you…
But our relationship is over and through.
So…
Maybe…
I will just start drinking hot chocolate with marshmallows.

2 Months Ago, 2 Day

2 months ago
2 day

We were kissing.

Kissing…
For a couple of more minutes and then we stopped.

We were talking.

2 months ago
2 day

We were talking about me being your "boo".

Canarsie is the nickname my cousin and I have for you.
I smile when I hear the songs by Lil Wayne and 50 Cent that you
dedicate to me.
I am so blinded by you; I cannot see anything clearly.

You talked about me being your "boo."
I acted like I didn't care.

When...

I really always wanted to hear this.

But...

I didn't let you know how much it affected me.

More kissing.

2 months ago
2 day

Now he's gone.

He's moved away.

Out of state.

I knew he was leaving.

But I didn't believe it.

Until he was gone.

Now I miss him.

I want to call him but I can't.

He's on my mind all the time.

I wish he was here with me.

All I have is the memories of...

2 months ago
2 day

When we were kissing…

2 months ago
2 day

When we were talking…

I didn't realize I was falling in love with him.

My Favorite Movie

Since 11 p.m. I've been writing poetry.
Now it's 11:15 p.m.;
I am still writing about you.

I miss you so much.
Your voice.
Your touch.
All in my head,
Replaying like my favorite movie.
I remember all of the things you said.

I want to cry because like NeYo said, *"I don't think that I can let go."*
I know you won't be coming back.
I know we won't be together.
I know things are not the same.
This is why I feel like I'm going insane.

I know that it's wrong.
But I continue to hold on.
Right now, I am laying in my bed.
With memories of you and me in my head.

The last time you were here in New York,

You showed me how much you really cared.

I wish I was talking to you,

On the phone...instead of being alone.

Since 11 p.m. I've been writing poetry.

Now it's 11:45 p.m.,

I am still writing about you.

I miss you so much.

Your touch.

Your voice.

All in my head,

Replaying like my favorite movie.

I remember all of the things you said.

I Thought

(Damn This Is the Boy I'm Looking For)

When he was with me,

It felt so good, like a real teenage love should.

I thought...*damn this is the boy I'm looking for*!

He was cute and dark-skinned,

Average height and even though I prefer tall boys I said, "He's an exception."

He had long hair,

Skin that felt so soft,

I thought...*damn this is the boy I'm looking for!*

He had a sweet voice

That put me in a trance.

Whenever he looked at me,

I thought...*damn this is the boy I'm looking for!*

Whenever we talked on the phone,

I thought...*damn this is the boy I'm looking for!*

Until I found out he wasn't looking for me!

Nubia

He claimed he did like me. He said,

"I like you a little bit."

I must be stupid. I guess I am because I let him in my heart.

I didn't know that he had a girlfriend and I was always the "side chick."

In the end he let me go, saying he was "sorry."

Blood rushing through my veins,

Feeling so much motherfucking pain!

Why me?

What did I do to deserve this feeling of being used?

I told him "No, we can't be friends."

I'm now thinking…

Damn!

Why the hell was I looking for him?

My Apology

Sorry, I care so much.

Sorry, I miss your touch.

Sorry, I want to be with you.

I am so sorry if I want you to want to be with me too.

Sorry, I love your kisses.

Sorry, you're the one I'm missing.

Sorry, for calling you.

Sorry, for wanting to hear your voice.

I am so sorry that you've always been my #1 choice.

Sorry, for liking you.

Sorry, for being me.

Sorry, for being kind.

I am so sorry for being sweet.

Sorry, for wanting you.

Sorry, I care so much.

I apologize for missing your touch.

Sorry, I want to be with you.

I am *so so* sorry if I want you to want to be with me too.

50/50

I'm caring about you,
But you don't care about me.

I want to be with you,
But you no longer want to be with me.

I'm holding on,
But you're letting go.

I call you,
But you don't answer the phone.

I cherish you, but you play me.

This is why you and I can no longer be.
Because our relationship is not 50/50.

Already Gone

My heart is heavy.

My heart feels like it's empty and gone.

The tears fall heavy from my eyes, like rain drops during a storm.

My mind is filled with memories of us.

I can't stop reminiscing.

It's your lips that I want to be kissing.

It's you that I am missing.

I don't want you to go, but like a person fleeing from a crime, you are already gone.

I am knocking—but you don't answer the door.

I am calling—but you ignore me as if I am chore on your list.

I feel dismissed.

But still I insist and I hold on.

I send a text message—but you don't respond.

I don't want you to go, but like fleeting time, you are already gone.

I say I love you, and I hear silence in response.

I want to be with you, but I am alone.

My mind is blown.

One part is tired of feeling used and says it's time to move on.

The other part clearly loves the emotional abuse and wants to hold on as long as it includes being with you.

I don't want you to go, but like a balloon slipping through my hands, you are already gone.

We were our best together.

We had our ups and downs.

You were always around.

I always thought we would be okay.

You had to know that no matter what you did I would stay and wait.

This all hurts.

I never wanted you to leave;

I never wanted you to go,

But like footprints washed away in the sand, you are already gone.

Problem

People say to me…
"You're so pretty",
"You're so smart",
But what am I to him?

How does he see me?
Am I ugly?
Stupid?
Annoying?
Maybe these are the reasons why he pushes me away,
While I beg for him to stay.
With him is where I want to be.
Unfortunately, he doesn't want to be with me.

I sit and wonder why…
Why can't I be *the one* in his eyes?

I take a minute to analyze my flaws,
Maybe it's because my hair isn't very long,
Maybe I'm too short,
Or too smart,
Maybe I annoy him,
I know I talk a lot!

I don't know,

I wonder why,

Tears continue to fall down my eyes...

I've been so focused on being with him,

That I lost the love I had for myself

by thinking that something was wrong with me!

When,

In actuality,

He is the one with the problem.

Part 5

Peddy

Do you remember your first puppy love? Your first puppy heartache? Your first major heartbreak? Young heartbreak can have your head up in the clouds as you sit on Brooklyn park benches and listen to the waves of water from the Brooklyn piers. You are a teenager; your brain isn't fully developed. My head was in the Brooklyn clouds as a teen, and I forgot about all of the special people on the ground in my life. After moving from Far Rockaway, Queens, my family and I, which now included my newly divorced single mother and my 4 younger siblings, had lived in several communities in Brooklyn including with relatives in Bed Stuy, across the street from my aunt in Flatbush, and in a predominately Jewish community in Crown Heights. My mother left an envelope filled with $4,000 of rent money on the counter of a local McDonalds as she ordered food for us. She was infamous in the family for misplacing important items. With the rent money gone, we returned to Halsey St. in Bed Stuy to live on the second floor of my grandmother's brownstone. It was a crowded home also occupied by my mother's two older brothers, but they made space as family often will in times of crisis. I found myself building a stronger relationship with my uncle Peddy as we lived together. He gave up his room for us and slept on the couch. I always knew who to call when I needed help, and he always came. I remember calling him after being punched in the face by a neighborhood boy. He arrived and put a caring arm around me. When I played Mariah Carey's love songs on repeat on my radio in my room, he decided that he had enough of me crying and he hid the CD. There was no Spotify or Apple music at that time, just the CD. I searched the house like crazy. I could not find it for a week. I felt miserable and my mother refused to buy me "The Emancipation of Mimi" album. She said she was tired of me crying too. I felt like no one understood me. I was going through my breakup phase and I needed to be soothed by the music of Mariah Carey. Peddy thought this was hilarious. He cracked jokes to make me laugh. He reminded me that life would go on…it did, and I survived. Sometimes we are so focused on the wrong people that we miss the precious moments with the right people in front of us. People who care for us, who love us for who we are, and who motivate us to be our best selves. We don't realize their impact on our lives until they are unexpectedly gone.

I still remember traveling on the B15 bus towards my best friend's house. The bus stopped at the intersection of Ralph and East New York Ave in Brownsville, Brooklyn. I got a call that my Uncle Peddy was dying at Kings County Hospital. He was admitted to the hospital after a fall and was expected to make a full recovery. I had just visited him. I let out an animalistic cry, and the bus driver stopped in the middle of the street and let me out. I rushed out as fast I could, one foot after the other and transferred to the B12 bus. I arrived at the hospital in East Flatbush, Brooklyn, and met my mom in the lobby with tears violently falling from my eyes. We ran into one of my close friends, who gave us a sympathetic hug. This was my mom's closest brother; it was extremely hard for her too. He had three young children who loved him immensely.

We all gathered to say goodbye. You couldn't speak but we were told that you could hear us. You left behind three children who were your world. I wish you could see them today. They are beautiful, talented, and every one of them looks exactly like you. I walked up to you at 16 years old, I hugged you as tight as I could, I cried and I said "I love you Peddy, I love you so much." My life would never be the same. I will never forget you. As a teenager I experienced my first grief, my first loss of family, my first experience with heart-break—my loss of you, through poetry.

To My Uncle

You'll make it through the rain.
You'll make it through the sleet.
You'll make it through the snow.
You'll make it through the cold.
You'll make it through the fall, winter, summer, and spring too.

All you have to do is look inside of you.
You'll make it if you want to.
All you have to do is try.
It may take time, but it will be worth the while.

I have faith in you.
I pray for you each day.
I ask God that you make it.
Because I love you,
I hope that you will be okay.

Please make it through this rain.
You don't need anyone's help.
All you need is yourself!

Do it for yourself!
Do it for your kids!
Your kids are the reason you live!

The Worse Pain

I never imagined that you would leave for good and never come back.

I stare at this obituary and collage of all of your pictures, and the tears just fall.
I feel like punching a wall.
More tears fall as "Trouble" by Jay-Z is heard on the CD player.
This is our song!
I have to tell you it's playing…

I look for you, but I can't find you.
I don't see you in your room,
In the kitchen,
On the computer,
Walking up the steps,
On the stoop,
Walking up the block,
Or sitting on the couch.
You're nowhere to be found on Halsey Street.

I don't hear the radio playing from your room.
I don't hear you on the phone or rapping.

I don't know where you are.

I wish you would come back.
I wish I could just see you smile, hear your laugh.

You were hilarious and protective; you were always there for me.

Every time I needed you, I called you and you were there!

Always making me feel beautiful and smart.
I miss you making fun of me being Grenadian and mocking my dad's accent.
I miss raping to Jay with you.
I miss talking to you and laughing with you.

This is the worse pain I've ever felt in my life.

Tears for Peddy

I wonder how you're doing.
I sit and stare at your pictures.
I can't believe you're really gone.

Why you?
You were my uncle!
Keeping secrets,
Talking with me,
Making me laugh,
I miss you.

You were always making fun of grandma,
Talking about how she's getting old and can't do dishes!
You were always cooking big breakfasts,
When your younger kids were over.
Those were my favorite mornings.
I admired the father you were to them.
I saw the love you had for them in each kiss, each hug, each laugh.

I miss you.
I love you.
I can't stop crying.
I kind of wish I was dying.

So, I could be with you.

I wish you could come back.

I don't know if I'll ever be able to deal with this pain.

Until we meet again,

I will always shed tears for Peddy.

Peddy

In 32 years, he blessed our lives,
Always by our side.
Helping with this, helping with that,
Peddy always had our back.

In my early childhood years, I remember always bothering him.
I'd ask "Where you going?"
He'd say "N.O.Y.B."
I'd say "Where's that, I want to go too!"
"None of your business," he'd reply.
Or when he had a car and he'd blast
"Mary Go Round" by Musiq Soulchild and "Song Cry" by Jay-Z,
Songs that now bring sadness to my life.

I remember us in the house on Halsey St.
Rapping to "Trouble" by Jay-Z.
Our favorite was the second verse,
"Respect me, I'm a thug!"

You were such a good person.
I just can't believe you're gone.

Why did God have to take you from me?

Somebody, please tell me, please,
Because I would like to know,
Why my uncle had to go.

The tears will never stop falling from my eyes,
Until you're back in my life.

I guess I will be crying forever,
Until the day we're back together.

Dear Peddy

I love you.

I miss you.

I wish I could get another chance to hug you and tell you I love you.

Because I do.

So much.

I miss you introducing me to your girlfriends as your favorite annoying niece.

I miss us laughing and cracking jokes in the kitchen.

I can see you looking me dead in my eyes saying,

"Nubia, you gonna make it, you gotta!"

I will.

I keep asking why God took my uncle.

I still can't answer that.

My Christian cousin says he needed him.

Why?

Doesn't he have other people?

Why did he need my uncle?

We needed my uncle!

We needed my uncle more than God!

I just want him back…
I doubt that'll be happening though,
It's wishful thinking.

I had another dream the other night.
My uncle just appeared and everyone was hugging him.
"What happened?" he asked.
He didn't know a thing.

I woke up happy.
My uncle was back.
I rushed to his room only to discover that he wasn't back at all.
That'll never change, and it *hurts so much*.

Part Six

Brooklyn Revolt

The loss of a loved one changes our lives in so many ways. Personally, it woke me up, it got my head out of the Brooklyn clouds. It helped me finally stand up on my own two feet and leave the park benches and piers of Brooklyn. I started to think about life outside of Brooklyn, which college I would attend and how I would contribute to the world. I decided to attend college out of New York State. I held a part-time job at a movie theatre in Brooklyn Heights, Brooklyn, during my summer breaks at home. It was there, in a dark movie theatre, that I met the most selfless young man who I would eventually date and marry. He, like my own father, immigrated to the United States at a young age. He was from Haiti, the first Black Republic in the world. It was a hard long-distance relationship, but we made it work.

My personal struggles led to my career in clinical social work, and I was proud to practice and serve my community in Brooklyn. Over time I became a wife and a mother to an Afro-Caribbean son. A new set of struggles began as I juggled these multiple roles. I found my way back to poetry. Poetry also helped me cope as an adult when my best friend, my first true love, my mother, was diagnosed with a rare form of cancer.

Our stories of struggle are personal but sharing these stories can be an act of revolt, a rising, a way to connect with others in our disconnected society currently dominated by internet relationships, selfies, and social media. It's a way to bring people together, a way to show others that they are not alone, it's a #metoo movement. There is no easy life. We are all overcoming our own individual, systematic, and institutionalized struggles. We are all survivors of something. The poetry that follows depicts my art, my ownership of my story, my experiences with love, uncertainty, change, and happiness, my rising, my Brooklyn Revolt.

All Things Come to an End

Stomach turning,
Kind of feels like butterflies.

Mind bending,
My head is spinning.

Nostalgic,
Reminiscing about everything...

Starting with the first time I mispronounced your Haitian name.
To the times that I didn't really like you.
To now...
When my feelings won't let me fight you.
I want you out of my head.

Instead,
You stay there.
You stay there as if it's your home or better yet...
Regal.

You're on my mind,
All of the time.
Text messages,
Instant messages,

I now can't wait to go to work,

To see your smirk,

To hear your sarcastic remarks.

You have an intelligent mind.

I'm at work thinking, *damn he's fine*

I would love for him to be all mine.

We're sitting in the movie theaters.

I'm waiting for a kiss.

I lay on your shoulder instead,

And wonder in my head,

Does he realize his touch sends chills down my body like adrenaline-spiked blood?

No instant message today.

My smile goes away.

I've been through so much pain in the past.

I just started focusing on myself, and I want our love to last.

I can't play myself.

I guess it was fun while it lasted, but I am tired of the same relation-ship games.

They say all good things that make you happy,

That make you smile,

That make you laugh,

Eventually...

It comes to an end.

Will this relationship be the same?

I Can

I can if I need to.
But do I need to?

I don't really want to.
But do you want me to?

Because if you want me to, I can.

I know I can give up, but I want to fight.
This feels so right.
You're all I think about at night.
And during the day.

I miss you every day that I'm away.

Problems are everywhere.

Long distance relationships are hard, but we should be able to beat it,
We should both want to beat it.

Together we can do it!

But, do you agree?

I can if I need to.
But do I need to?

I don't really want to.
But do you want me to?
Because if you do want me to…
Because if there's no other way…
Because if it's the best thing to do…
I can let go and move on from you.
But I don't want to.

Perfect

Perfect?

What is perfection?

Does it mean with you there are no tears shed?

No pain felt?

Constant happiness?

Perfect?

What is perfection?

Does it mean you're flawless?

Flawless personality?

Flawless skin?

Flawless beauty?

Does it mean you're flawless within?

Perfect?

What is perfection?

Does it mean that you've never hurt someone?

Never broke their heart?

That you cared for them and loved them right from the start of the relationship?

Until the end?

Wait…

If you're perfect...does the relationship ever end?

Are there arguments?

Are there phone slams?

Are there silent treatments?

You have that "good guy" label,

But you're far from perfect.

You don't know everything, but you swear you do.

You don't always say what's on your mind.

You don't always stay true to you.

You've hurt people in the past.

You don't always show you care.

You're uncertain about many things.

You're not a good listener.

Or good at giving compliments.

You have that "good guy" label.

I'm honestly able to say you're not a "bad guy."

But you're far from perfect.

I'm not perfect either,

But we can still give our love a try.

Perfection doesn't exist.

It's a myth.

It's unattainable.

Our relationship will not be perfect.

But if we fight for it, it will be worth it.

30 Reasons Why

Your smile.

Your arms.

Your dance.

Your commitment to your family.

How much you love me.

Your selfishness.

The way you sleep.

How awesome of a cook you are.

The fact that this love started with a book.

Oh, and the movies, of course.

You always get me dessert.

You catch me in my lies.

You forgive me when I'm wrong.

You hold me when I cry.

You're strong.

You're funny.

You're a great person.

You watch weird shows.

You know all the elevator music in every store.

You see through all my bullshit.

You call me out when I need it.

You're always there for me.

You love me for no reason.

Nubia

You wear sunglasses no matter the season.

Me being with anyone else would feel like treason.

When I want you to leave, you stick around.

Our son looks just like you.

I'm proud of the man you've become.

I've been with you since you were 19.

I'm grateful to have you.

You're my husband, and the father of our son.

I love you and these were 30 reasons why.

Happy 30th birthday baby;

I hope all of your dreams come true.

I am so blessed to be on this life journey with you.

To My Son

You are a ball of energy.
You are the light of my life.
I love watching you sleep at night.

Your smile...
So bright and carefree.
It erases all of the worries within me.

Your hair...
An Afro that is large.
You are so cool.
I see you as a reflection of me, yet you are still you.

Your laughter...
Makes my heart melt.
It's one of my favorite sounds.
I love having you around.

My first born,
My son,
You have turned our house into a home,
And made us a family of 3.

You're special and loved so much by your daddy and me.

I am so grateful for you.

I know you will do great things.

The world will see.

Just remain happy, kind, loving and free!

Black Lives Matter

I look in your eyes.

You look in mine.

You're so full of wonder.

You're so divine.

I give you a hug and feel the warmth of your Chocolate Brown skin.

You have a beautiful smile.

An Afro.

And you are filled with the most joyous laughter.

A child of this world.

You're almost 3.

It's hard to believe,

And sometimes I don't want to see…

What's ahead for you as a young Black man?

I know you'll experience relationships and love.

But the other possible experiences I don't want to see or believe that they could happen in this century.

Your family are immigrants from Haiti and Grenada.

Your family were sharecroppers in Alabama.

They all migrated to New York, to Brooklyn.

Identifying as African American in this White America.

This society will just see you as Black.

All some people will see is your skin…

Not any of your values, goals, or who you are within.

No matter what rules you follow or laws you don't break…

They'll make up their own stereotypes,

One wrong look and your life they can take.

Without a second thought you can be jailed or harassed,

By some people paid to protect and serve

Or by some people who feel like what you're doing is getting on their nerves.

Jordan Davis was killed because a White man thought his music was too loud.

Trayvon Martin was killed because another man thought he shouldn't be on his side of the town.

It's clear…

Some people don't see little Black boys as human.

George Floyd was murdered by a White cop's knee after being pinned to the ground.

Ahmaud Aubrey was shot and killed while jogging.

Tamir Rice was shot and killed in a park with a toy gun he was holding.

There are so many Black lives that have been lost unjustly, to list them all, would take cataloguing.

I worry about you so much.

Being a Black man in America can be a death sentence.

I pray that this doesn't happen to my son.
Or anyone else's son.
Sometimes prayers can go unanswered.
I'll just keep shouting that all of our Black Lives Matter!

Tired

I am so tired.

I could really cry.

I try but sometimes…

I feel so sad.

And so mad.

About how much I give.

And how much people take.

Worrying so much about everyone I love,

Trying to take care of everything,

As a wife, social worker, mother.

Always putting others before myself.

When does it stop?

I don't want it to go on.

I need some rest.

I want to feel my best.

I don't want to be tired.

I need some help!

It's time to go to therapy and to focus on myself.

Sometimes

Sometimes I want to pull out my hair!

Sometimes I don't care.

Sometimes I feel alone.

Sometimes I'm in my own zone.

Sometimes I feel like I'm on my own.

Sometimes I want to cry.

Sometimes I want to hide.

I feel like I can't breathe.

Like something is wrong with me.

I know my doctor diagnosed me with postpartum depression,

But I feel like I could use a new brain!

The one I have leads me to feel so much stress and makes my life feel like a mess.

Sometimes I can't rest.

Sometimes I want to scream!

Sometimes I wonder about the real me and if I'm being a good mom to my kid,

Wife to my husband,

A person to me.

Sometimes I just want to *be*…

Do you ever feel like this sometimes?

Under-Potentialize

In college I was earning a 4.0 GPA,

Chasing academic perfection,

Never reaching it because it doesn't exist.

Feeling stressed,

Sometimes depressed.

A professor turned to me and said, "If you don't let go of perfection, you're going to

Under-Potentialize yourself."

As an adult I now wonder…

Have I Under-Potentialized myself?

Could I be more in life?

More than a wife?

More than a mom?

More than a social worker?

Is there more out there for me?

Is there someone else I could be?

Additional roles I could fulfill?

More for me to do?

They say women can't have it all!

Have I chosen motherhood over my career?

I know after I had my son all I wanted was for him to be near me.

Career aspirations were set aside.

Mom guilt,

Postpartum depression,

Were my new reality.

Being a perfect mom was all I wanted to be.

But perfection doesn't exist!

I used to believe I would give my all to my career with no children near.

But now I have a son.

So...

Did I Under-Potentialize myself?

Now...

I continue to grow as a wife, mom, and a social worker.

I'm a person.

I now realize I didn't Under-Potentialize myself.

Under-Potentialize is not even a real word.

I still continue to grow.

And I am starting to see that there is more to me.

I am more than this word.

And, most importantly, I am more than what I do.

I am more than roles fulfilled.

I am more than a wife.

I am more than a mom.

I am more than a social worker.

I can just be.

I can just be me.

Brooklyn Runner

One step.

Two steps.

Three steps.

Four.

Stressed.

Overwhelmed.

In danger.

Out the door.

5 a.m. in the summer and spring.

6 a.m. in the winter and fall.

With my Asics,

Compression tights and tee,

I am running down the streets of Brooklyn,

Feeling free.

It's something about looking up at the sky,

While your sneakers lightly hit the pavement.

It's something about looking up at the clouds,

And the green leaves on the trees,

That reminds me to just be!

I don't always have to do.

It gives me perspective,

Reminds me that the world is bigger than me!

Running in Brooklyn helps clear my mind when I can't see.

Life is foggy at times.

I don't like to run with anyone,

But sometimes I do enjoy running with my son.

I can run away from my problems even for a brief time.

I can have a space away from home that is just mine.

Out in my Asics,

Compression tights and tee,

I am running down the streets of Brooklyn,

Feeling free.

I'm feeling free while running through...

East Flatbush,

Brownsville,

Bed Stuy,

To Brooklyn Bridge Park,

Park Slope,

Prospect Park,

Brooklyn Heights,

Running through memories of life,

Feeling like I can overcome any strife with every one of my strides.

I may not be the best,

But when running, you don't have to better than the rest.

It's a sport where your competition is you!

I make the rules, the pace, the route.

I choose my own journey.

It's me against me.

Running half and full marathons,

I trained myself into an athlete.

Motherhood,

Work,

Being a wife,

The overall stressors of life could never take me away from running.

I'm a Brooklyn runner for life.

Forgiveness

Can I forgive others for actions committed in the past?

Can I forgive myself?

Can I move on or will this pain last?

I'm usually okay,

But today has been rough.

I keep thinking of my struggles and hurt.

I find my thoughts focused on the past.

Thinking how could I do this?

How could I do that?

How could I let myself get so hurt?

I'm better than that!

Everything happens for a reason,

This I know.

Without these experiences...

I don't know how my life would be or what would have happened to me.

So, I choose to forgive myself,

And others for the past.

It's the first step to get my sanity back.

I choose to accept all of me...

The good.

The bad.

The ugly.

Things I wanted that were out of my grasp,

Led me to the life I currently have,

And for that I appreciate all of the experiences I have had in my life.

I choose to forgive.

I choose to send loving-kindness to my past.

I practice self-compassion.

I do it for me.

I do it to set myself free.

Alright

"Are you alright?"
Is what you ask me.
Even though you're the one who is sick,
You still look out for me.
That's the person you are.
Emotionally and physically suffering but still looking out for others.

Why is this happening to you?
Is something I still wonder and ponder…

I don't want to bother you with my trivial life,
While you're fighting for yours.
So…
I say, "I'm alright."

Even though
I cry for you every night.
I pray for you every day.

The truth is…
Nothing for me will be alright.
Life for me will not be the same.
My days will be filled with gray
Until you are physically okay.

Brooklyn Revolt (Dear Mama)

Headache.

Tears falling down my cheeks.

Can't sleep.

Don't want to get out of bed or eat.

Constantly asking why...

Why my mom?

A question that can't be answered because terrible shit just happens

In

Life.

Days turn into nights.

There's no denying

The emotional pain

Or physical strain of the stress,

Of the nightmares of your possible death,

Of feeling like I can't go on,

Of feeling so alone.

But.

Then.

I talk to you.

And I realize that for a minute,

I was unaware,

I literally forgot,

That you're still here!

Your presence today in our lives is a **blessing**!

Dear Mama

You're filled with so much positivity.

You're standing strong in winds of uncertainty.

If you can cope,

If you have hope,

Then so can I.

It may be hard but I tell myself that I can at least try

For

You.

I can let myself feel my emotions and provide you with support.

I can be positive and remind myself that life is out of my control.

As much as I want to protect you,

There's nothing about this cancer diagnosis that I can do.

All I can do it be here for you.

And I will.

Together we will take this one day at a time.

We will find the strength within.

To fight this battle.

And love each other and appreciate the gift of life and peace.

We will fight this together as a family.

It's one of the many fights of your life.

It's another fight.

It's another struggle that you take in stride.

It's another challenge that you will overcome.

Dear Mama

I know you will revolt,

I know you will rise,

And I will be right here by your side.

Reframe

Whatever struggles you've experienced…
Whatever you've been through,
Will not get the best of you!

You thought life would be easy!
But the Universe, God, Jehovah, Allah,
Whatever is your faith…
Put a struggle right in your face.

Your life's struggle,
Whatever it is,
Or *Struggles,*
Whatever they are,
Will **not** beat you!

In spite of your life's struggles,
You will push through,
And here you are today,
You overcame your struggles…
You made your own way!

Realizing your life
Is what it is.

Brooklyn Revolt

You are who you are

Because you **overcame** struggles in life.

So whatever struggles are ahead,

Because struggles don't go away,

Because more are sure to come,

Struggles either get upgraded or exchanged,

Whatever is ahead…

Just know you got it!

You're resilient.

You're one in a million.

These struggles will give you strength,

In the battle of life.

You were built for this.

You can and will win against life's challenges.

Mommy & Daddy

My 3-year-old son fell and hurt himself.

He cried out in pain.

He constantly yelled out "Daddy!" in between tears.

When we're in pain, we call out for our parents.

So many Black lives have been unjustly lost in this country.

So many Black voices have called out for their parents while being unjustly killed by others.

Most times their voices fell on deaf ears.

I pray for all my young Black boys and girls, young Black Trans people too!

I never wanted a son.

It is my worse fear…

For my son to call my name out in pain while being attacked because he's Black.

We have been through so much as a people.

But we're strong, because our ancestors are strong!

Because our mothers and fathers are strong!

Because we are the children of our mothers and fathers and our ancestors!

We can call out in pain, and we can still be strong.

We can also call out...
Mommy and Daddy!

While they are here,
While we share this earth,
We can show gratitude and love to the two people who loved us most.
We won't just call out in pain!
We will revolt, we will rise.
We won't just call out in pain or during our demise.
We will call to share happiness, to share love, to share growth.

To my Mommy and Daddy...
I love you!
I am the woman I am, the parent I am, the person I am... because of you two!
Thank you for always putting me first!
Thank you for showing me that you cared!
Thank you for always being there!

Thank You

Endless tears at night…

Experiencing pain that feels like there is no end in sight.

Thinking that something about me is not right.

Blaming myself for childhood trauma,

Heartbreak,

Lost friendships,

And family problems too.

Instead of turning my back to these feelings,

I now face and acknowledge these feelings,

I now accept,

I now revolt,

I now rise,

I now say, thank you!

Thank you to the doors of new opportunities that were slammed in my face.

Thank you to the shoes of people I cared about who walked away.

Thank you to the relationships I thought I wanted the most.

Thank you to the sexual trauma I experienced as a young girl.

I needed all to become me,

And I am grateful to all of you for…

Giving me strength,

Showing me love,

Pushing me to grow,

For being a part of my life,

At one point or the other,

For a season or a reason,

I wouldn't have it any other way...

Thank you!

Without you,

I wouldn't be who I am today.

Afterword

Writing poetry has helped me grow in life.

I started this project of self-reflection in the summer of 2020. While reviewing my poetry and journals, several themes emerged and provided a clear structure to this collection. I began to write new material as a way to cope with the COVID-19 pandemic, the continued unjust killing of African Americans in this country, and my mom's cancer diagnosis. This project of self-reflection transformed into my own personal celebration of poetry. Thank you for reading. I hope you find your own creative outlet, your own positive way to cope, your own way to overcome your challenges in life. I hope you keep rising and that you continue to revolt.

About Author

Nubia is a clinical social worker who was raised in Brooklyn, NY, where she currently lives with her husband and son. "Brooklyn Revolt" is her debut narrative poetry collection. When she is not sharing precious moments with her family, she enjoys reading, writing, meditating, running, yoga and spending time outdoors.

Made in the USA
Columbia, SC
31 January 2021

32031923R10070